The Geometry of Business Ethics

Patrick Henz

CONTENTS

Acknowledgments   i

1   Introduction   1

2   The Fraud Triangle   19

3   Evolution of the Triangle   49

4   Bibliography   51

5   About the Author   53

ACKNOWLEDGMENTS

The book is based on the "Fraud Triangle", a theoretical model presented in 1973 by the US sociologist and criminologist Donald Cressey. Born in 1919, he obtained his bachelor's degree from Iowa State College in 1943 and seven years later his doctorate from Indiana University. Most of his life he spent in California, where taught sociology at the University of California in Santa Barbara.

Together with Edwin Sutherland he wrote in 1934 "Principles of Criminology", what should become a standard text. After his retirement he stayed active in the field of white-collar crime. Beside becoming the president of the Institute for Financial Crime Prevention, he published later the famous theory of the "Fraud Triangle".

1 INTRODUCTION

Welcome to the Geometry of Compliance and thanks for taking your time to read this! This book is not a Compliance manual or how-to-do document, but shows Compliance in relation to business- & social-psychology and further the sustainability concept. Doing so, it is made for the advanced practitioner and includes the following:

- The Cost of Information
- The Fraud Triangle

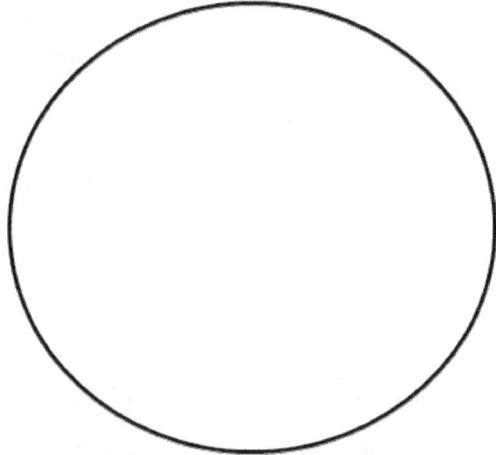

1.1 But first a step back, why we should care about business ethics?

An interesting quote by US author and philosopher Ayn Rand, taken from her masterpiece, the novella "Atlas Shrugged":

"When you see that trading is done, not by consent, but by compulsion – when you see that in order to produce, you need to obtain permission from men who produce nothing – when you see that money is flowing to those who deal, not in goods, but in favors – when you see that men get

richer by graft and by pull than by work, and your laws don't protect you against them, but protect them against you – when you see corruption being rewarded and honesty becoming a self-sacrifice – you may know that your society is doomed."[1]

"Atlas Shrugged" plays in a near future post-recession United States, ruled by a kind of socialistic government, including cartels and corruption. Result is further negative development of the country. The two main characters are business leaders of railroad and steel companies and start to fight the system.

The novella is based on Amy's philosophy of objectivism and published back in 1957. Besides that the book was controversial discussed by critics, it reached fame and even got movie-adaptions. Nevertheless of its age, "Atlas Shrugged" and the mentioned quote are still alarming actual and relevant.

So why corrupt societies are doomed or in other words, what is the cost of corruption?

For the company:

- Corruption (as part of missing legal certainty) is an additional cost factor. The tasks of the employees are not just limited in elaborating the best technical solutions, finding an adequate pricing, but also have to deal with local bureaucracy and connections. These costs are included in the decision making process, in which countries a company wants to expand and invest. As corruption destroys legal certainty, it opens the "casino risk", as there are no guarantees that with the bribe you win the project and there stays the risk of getting caught.

[1] Rand, Ayn (1957): "Atlas Shrugged"

- "Financial incentives may lure the more talented and better educated to engage in rent seeking rather than in productive work, with adverse consequence for the country's growth rate."[2]

- Corruption reduces the efficiency of the public sector and money "gets lost on the way": Due to the missing effectiveness in its processes, the country on the one hand loses the possibility of receiving the totality of the taxes; and on the hand, the costs of public investments increase.

- With given corrupt structures, a public buyer will look for its best personal benefit (including the possibility of receiving a bribe), which is normally not compatible with the best public benefit. Further consequence: "Corruption may distort the composition of government expenditure. Corruption may tempt government officials to choose government expenditures less on the basis of public welfare than the opportunity they provide for extorting bribes."[3]

- As quality of infrastructure, education and healthcare are arguments to compete with other countries to receive the needed foreign direct investments, countries with a high corruption level are less attractive for global companies. Less investment means smaller budgets and less competitive products. This fosters the results that budget for infrastructure, education and healthcare is missing. As education does not only mean teaching of knowledge, but also of values, it is difficult for a society to break this cycle.

At the end Ayn Rand's philosophy and theories as from Paulo Mauro fit perfectly together with actual statistics.

---

[2] Mauro, Paulo (1997): „Why worry about Corruption?"
[3] Mauro, Paulo (1997): „Why worry about Corruption?"

Again, why should we care about business ethics?

Erich Gutenberg defines in his "principle of profit" that corporations in a market-based system are striving for to maximize their profit, based on the used resources, on the long-run.[4] Corruption reduces the return on investment as it reduces the earnings. Potential suppliers bribe the employees of the procurement department with the consequences that our company does not receive the best quality for the price. On the other hands I have to share my profit with governmental officials, who are requesting a bribe. Beside additional costs, this includes a certain "casino risk": the possibility that your bribe and nevertheless not win the project and / or that you get caught violating the law. The last possibility can have consequences until the closing of the company.

As corruption is not just an additional tax for the company, but also for all citizens, it reduces the motivational factor of the salary, as in fact a part of it get lost to the need of regular non-formal payments. Further as company you cannot be sure, if you really have the best employees or only the ones with the best relations to their teachers and professors.

Why care?

Gutenberg's definition is not the only truth. Not all companies had been founded with the pure idea to maximize profit. A lot of times the founder was an engineer or inventor with a product or idea, in what he or she believed, not just to sell, but to satisfy a need and bring on the development of the society. At least for this first generation of management, the company had always also a social responsibility. This carried on, as the founder's spirit gets immortalized in the company's values and code of conduct. Later generations of managers continued with social aspects, as there are economic reasons for that:

---

[4] Gutenberg, Erich (1979): "Grundlagen der Betriebswirtschaftslehre, Band 1: Die Produktion

A good corporate citizen is regarded in society and politics. It supports the company's lobbying and avoids the implementation of higher taxes and / or more strict processes, especially for companies which produce goods, which not always compatible with public welfare.

In the '81 movie "Blade Runner" the Nexus 7-android Roy Batty explained to the computer genius J.F. Sebastian: *"We're not computers, Sebastian, we're physical."*

- Even if employees work , first of all, to receive a salary, they feel an inner need to be proud of their-selves, which includes the company which they are working for, as they spend a relevant time of the day there. "Proud to work for this company" is a non-tangible part of the salary. An important factor, especially for employees, which are already on a higher level on Maslow's pyramid. If this motivational factor is not available, the company has to substitute it with higher salaries.

- To maximize economic rent-seeking, employees do not spend anymore their work time for their official tasks, but to execute and hide the bribery. As this is against personal values and interests, their level of motivation goes down and the company's sick leave level up.

- If corruption is wide-spread in a society and employees do not have the possibility change to a transparent company, they stay where they are, but mentally quit. The company loses potential, especially on the global market, where they compete against transparent companies.

- Further this means a deviation to company's core values and code of conduct, as most entities define here their sustainability vision and the wish to be perceived as a good global citizen. If the company not consequently protects its values, this can be the start of a lingering corrosion.

Most probably corruption would start at the company's both ends, sales and procurement; meaning bribing or getting bribed. For instance, it can start with a sales employee, with a small bribe or a facilitation payment.

Corruption is learnt and if to such action follows a positive result, the employee learnt it as a successful behavior and may extend its usage. This will not be limited on his or her behavior regarding external stakeholders, but will continue with by-passing first the most bureaucratic internal process and later others. The relevant factor for business success is now sales and its relations to potential clients, what includes bribery. As consequence, the importance of production and procurement goes down. Cost pressure will hit the production side, as quality leadership is not required. Further procurement loses its independence, as the informal sales-client-relations will need concessions, as the usage of providers, which are recommended by the customer. Similar to a public society, corruption slowly crawls through all areas of the company. The results get perceived by all employees, as hopefully someone will use an internal or external whistle blower-hotline. If not, the corrosion continues.

Even if the company is purely focused on profit, the single employee is not. As consequence, a company has to take on social responsibility, which starts with obeying to the law, human rights and goes on to foundations and social events.

As discussed, corruption weakens the competitiveness of the company, but on the other hand, similar to a cartel, corruption reduces the free competition and can lead to monopolies and nearly monopolies. Lambsdorff showed in his '98 study "that exporters from less corrupt countries face disadvantages in import countries with a high corruption level."[5] This can have three reasons:

1) The company has not the required experience or local connections.
2) The company understands the sustainability concept
3) The company wants or has to comply with local and global laws, as the FCPA or UKBA

---

[5] Dreher, Axel / Herzfeld, Thomas (2005): "The Economic Costs of Corruption: A Survey and New Evidence

Even if on the long run corrupt behavior will turn against the company, on a short run this can mean an advantage, as corrupt companies in countries with a high corruption level can us these market limitations to earn higher profits. This makes it clear that cost of corruption are not the sum of the bribery payments, but the development of the region, as clients not get the best quality for their money. This can include basic products, but also affects product safety (including public projects) or healthcare solutions. So it is no surprise that Matthew Murray and Andrew Spalding analyzed, if freedom from official corruption can and / or should be a human right.[6]

The Bertelsmann Stiftung elaborates the "Sustainable Governance Indicators. As part of them, they measure the "Quality of Democracy", an index, what includes the electoral process, access to information, civil rights & political liberties and rule of law, for the OECD-countries.[7] If we compare this 2014 index against the Transparency International Corruption Perception Index 2014[8], we get a good positive correlation of 0,68.

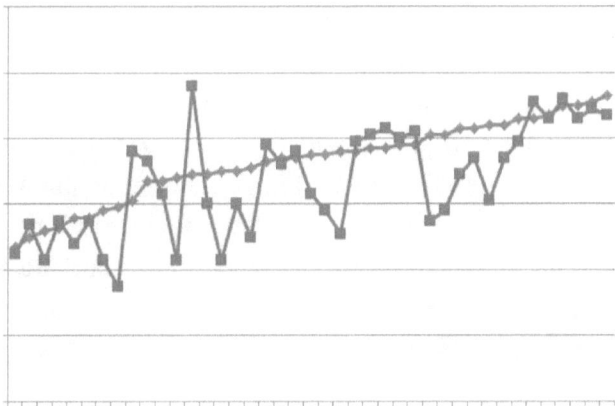

---

[6] Murray, Matthew / Spalding (2015): "Freedom from Official Corruption as a Human Right"
[7] Sustainable Governance Indicators (2014): "Quality of Democracy"
[8] Transparency International (2014): "Corruption Perception Index"

As this is a statistical relation, it does not determine if corruption lowers the quality of democracy or the other way around. Based on Donald Cressey's Fraud Triangle we can assume that it is a vicious circle, as non-efficient bureaucracy provokes bribery and missing transparency inside a company can corrupt the public institutions.

These costs not only affect the citizens of a corrupt country, but people around the world. As for example, a company can use the strong position in a corrupt country to reach higher margins and profits and thanks to this, to acquire their transparent competitors, and limit further competition, not just on a regional market, but also on global level.

The "UN Brundtland Report" defines sustainability as *"meeting the needs of the present without compromising the ability of future generations to meet their one needs."*[9] Seen as this, sustainability was interpreted from an economic point of view by Erich Gutenberg and his "principle of profit", as corporations in a market-based system are striving for to maximize their profit, based on the used resources, on the long-run.

Most companies understand this to use natural resources with care, so that they continue to exist also for tomorrow's generations. Further its neighbors are important, as good citizens it is imperative to support the community. This is not limited to found schools or plant trees, but includes that the company is not just today working efficiently, but does the same tomorrow and beyond. With this it can continue to support the community, be a source for local tax-income and stay available to offer jobs for local people.

A long-term strategy based on the company's vision and values is required! But this alone is not sufficient to ensure the future results. Guidelines and processes have to be implemented, if not it would be a

---

[9] Brundland, Gro Harlem (1987): "Our common future", part of the Brundtlandreport

pure accident to reach the company's targets. Surely it is possible to find short-cuts and win projects with ignoring laws and regulations. But most of the times, there are just victories on the short run. Maybe not at once, but years later such deviations get discovered. The results are high fines, loss of reputation and can even include black-listing. Not to talk that the cost of corruption are paid by all. Corruption not only brings the company down, but with it the local community.

A company needs the will to accomplish its vision. For this all employees have to walk in the same direction to reach this goal. Compliance ensures that the company's vision is lived and respected; it is the will to create great things together.

Values + Strategy + Compliance = Sustainability

This is valid in a theoretical environment, where we have complete information. In reality our information is incomplete, in private and business life are always surprises to be expected. For this we need to be prepared for the unprepared. Our strategy must be able to handle unforeseen opportunities. The same is valid for an ethics & compliance program, as processes, guidelines and IT tools have to give the employee flexibility to answer the sudden opportunities of the market. This to avoid the temptation that employees try to bypass such internal processes. Further it is an important task of the company to prepare its employees to such situations. Several pressures are working together:

- Most employees (as sales department) have ambitious annual targets. A surprisingly appearing opportunity often seems to be the only possibility to reach them.
- People assume that such opportunities could disappear as fast as they appeared. For this sudden opportunities tend people to act fast and bypass their normal decision making process.
- Depending on a person's character, employees overestimate their possibility to control a situation. This is especially true for

"success seekers", they tend to overestimate their own abilities and underestimate the risks of the situation. For the "failure avoiders" it is the other way around. Thanks to self-selection the first group of people will try to get more risky tasks with the goal that they can prove their selves and advance faster in their career, they will apply to positions in sales or become a race driver. In sudden and new projects they see the opportunity, but not the risk.

Compliance has to be aware of such psychological effects, which can lead to ethical blindness. Counter measures can be implemented, as trainings & workshops, but also a strong position of the Compliance Officer is required, who has to be a trusted business adviser. White elephants are a big risk. A company may wrongly calculate the business risks, as costs are higher than expected, the company's experience and products are not adequate or also the potential attractive project got won with bribery. This leads us to an updated formula:

Values (fixed) + Strategy (flexible) + Compliance (flexible) = Sustainability

To offer the required flexibility and with this value for the business, Compliance cannot limit itself to approve or not approve, but if something is not possible, it has to be analyzed, if the same result can be reached via a different route. Most employees do not want to do something forbidden, but maybe not had been aware of the risks and specific regulations. Here the Compliance tasks are to adapt the related action, so that it complies with all laws and regulations. A good example is the mixture between GPS and social network: "Waze". This App, available for Android and iPhone, tells the user the quickest way from point A to B, this is not always the shortest way, but also traffic and even police controls, construction sites or accidents play a role. Just as the app, the Compliance Officer guides the way through the unknown territory and keeping the employee on the legal paths; changing legal realities on the radar.

1.2 The Cost of Information

As the "normal employee" may not be that highly engaged in ethics & compliance as the Compliance Officer (or other kind of Compliance expert), it is a relevant question how much it costs to get the Compliance information to decide if you want to include it in your decision taking or not.

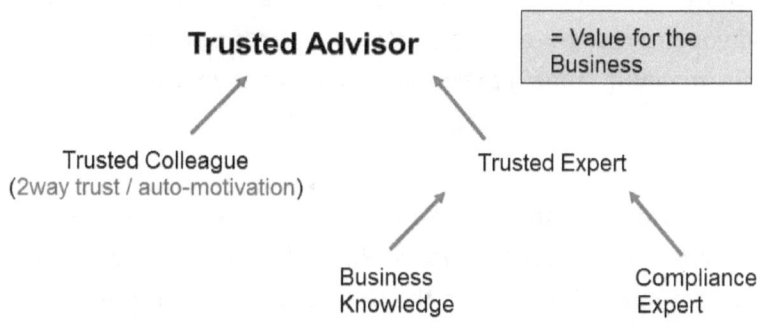

Adapted from the Communicator Model (Market Psycology)

The goal for a Compliance Officer (as all other Compliance employees) should be to be recognized as a "trusted advisor". This includes two sub-roles, being a trusted expert, but also a trusted colleague. It makes no sense being the biggest Compliance expert, if you have no idea about the business and how the company is earning the money. Also visibility is needed so that employees can see their Compliance Officer as a trusted colleague, who is not just talking about Compliance, but living it as a good example. Here it is helpful not see everybody as a potential risk, but starting from the idea that more than 99% of the employees are good and honest people, making daily their best effort for the company. These people are to be protected and prepared so that they will not get into trouble via accident (or through a case caused by the less than 1% black sheep, which you may have).

With this view, Compliance can be seen as a part of a "0 harm culture", as most companies have implemented. Also you should control your auto-motivation from time to time. A Compliance department is always a service for the business side. To be seen as a trusted expert, you must have certain business knowledge to understand the colleagues and their needs. Visiting plants and / or project sites are very important, not just to understand how the technology is working, but also how the employees are thinking. If trusted expert and colleague came together and you are recognized as a trusted advisor, employees will invest more costs (meaning "time") to contact you and get your opinion.

Most of the companies have more than just one site, but Compliance centralized in the head-quarters. With this we have the situation that a lot of employees do not see the Compliance Officer in their daily work, but maybe once or twice a year, when Compliance training is scheduled. But you can use the local manpower to install a Compliance Ambassador or Champion. A trusted colleague, who with the help of regular Compliance trainings can take the position of a local assessor, this means respond to basic questions, but most of all, being a first face of Compliance, a figure, who others talk to, if they have a topic. Here it is not important that this champion or ambassador can directly respond to all questions, but being a link between the site and the Compliance Officer in headquarters. Having such a role implemented is reducing the costs of information, as a local employee do not have to contact somebody from outside and talk with someone, who is not known; but having a local trusted advisor, who is always accessible.

1.3 *"It is easier to resist at the beginning than at the end"*: A Compliance Lesson by Leonardo da Vinci

In the province of Florence you can find the small city of Vinci. Today around 14,300 citizens are living here. More than 500 years ago, Leonardo was born near this place and based on the tradition, received his name "Leonardo di ser Piero da Vinci". As universal genius, talented artist and curious in all aspects, he became the ideal of the Renaissance time.

In his famous "Vitruvian Man" he realistically pictured a man from different angles, but Leonardo not only understood the outside, also human psychology, as his quote "It is easier to resist at the beginning than at the end" shows. Being in the beginning of a potential Compliance risk is the best time to contact your Compliance Officer. An individual will do this if his or her benefit will be higher than the investments.

Definitions:

r) Estimated Compliance Risk: The estimated negative impact for company

b) Anticipated Benefit of Compliance: The estimated positive impact of the Compliance to solve the problem

c) Cost of Information: The estimated cost to contact the Compliance Officer and / or to involve him or her. This includes also an estimated negative or positive impact for the employee, for example potential disciplinary action or an award for whistleblower. For the last case the cost would turn into benefit.

$$(1/r) > b - c$$

An employee, who received Compliance training, will guess how big a Compliance risk may be. As he or she is not an expert on the topic, this estimation can be right, but also wrong. If the Compliance department will be contacted depends now, how the benefit of this is anticipated by the employee and how cost-intensive is receiving relevant Compliance information and decisions. If the 1/"estimated risk" is assumed to be higher than the anticipated benefit minus the costs to receive this information, the employee will not seek to contact Compliance. As the risk estimation can be wrong, this can lead to a Compliance problem; a relevant risk for the company.

$$(1/r) < b - c$$

On the other hand, if benefit minus costs is still higher than the 1/"estimated risk"; Compliance will be involved. So these are the four factors, with which can be worked on:

- Foster employees' Compliance knowledge so that they able to judge correctly potential risks.
- Make Compliance a trusted advisor which can offer relevant information. This maximized the anticipated benefit of Compliance involvement.
- Lower the cost of information. Compliance must be close to the business and easy to reach. Additionally an award for positive behavior up to for whistleblower can be implemented. If possible tools as smart phones and apps should be used to ensure communication availability 24 hours and 7 days a week.
- Connect Compliance with company and personal values. With this a potential wrong-doing will lead to pressure inside the employee, as (potential) actions not are compatible with own attitudes and values. Lowering psychological pressures would be another benefit of Compliance involvement.

Just as Leonardo predicts, the longer you are walking down on the wrong path, the more difficult it gets to resist the future wrong doing, as with the time the cost of information gets higher. This includes that first of all, the employee has to admit his personal failure and also has to assume that now the correct behavior will be paired with a smaller or bigger disciplinary action.

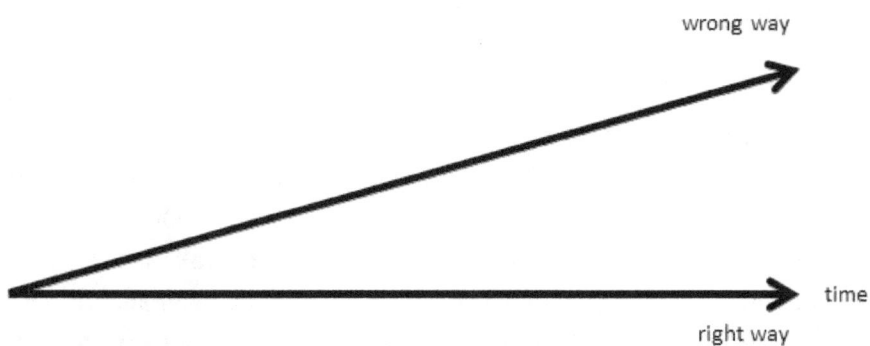

Perception is important. The employee has to understand that he or she is on the wrong way. In many cases this is not the case right from the beginning. The employee perceives him or herself as on the right way, but then more or less suddenly understands that this is not the case. Hereby can perception be everywhere in between the absolute black and white. Through the employee's eyes he or she can be one any imagine imaginable path on or above the right one, even above the wrong way.

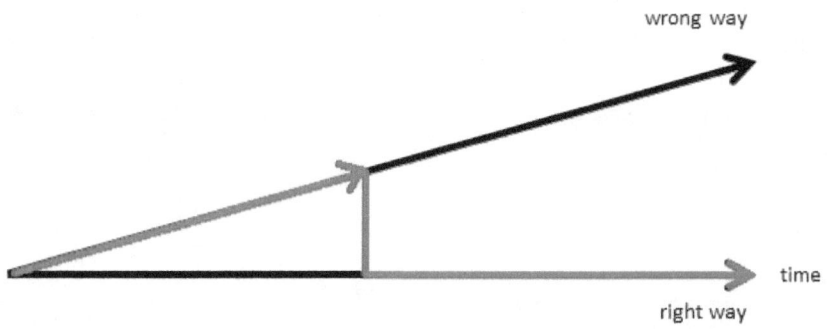

Again, Compliance trainings support employees not just to stay on the right way, but also if they left this path, to recognize this as early as possible. Here such a workshop cannot limit itself on pure teaching of information, but must include real-life case discussions and psychological stress situations, which may lead to the ethical blindness-phenomenon.

According to Leonardo, it is easier to resist a future wrong-doing (=continuing to walk down the wrong path), if you are still in the beginning, at or soon after a decision. This because the longer you are on the wrong way, the bigger gets the gap and the more difficult to jump from the wrong to the right path. Meaning, if you want to return on the right way, you have to communicate with your Compliance Officer and a) commit your wrong-doing to yourself and b) to the company. Most organizations have a range of disciplinary actions, which starts from nothing, if it is plausible that the deviation was a pure accident, up to separation of the employee from the company, if it is a sever case. The cost of information gets higher with the time. But there can be also negative costs, if there is an whistleblower ward.

Based on Leonardo we include "g = gap" in our calculation:

$$(1/r) < b - c - g$$

Herby the gap is defined as:

v) Own responsibility for wrong-doing

s) Severity of the wrong decision (the angular degree between both paths)

t) Time

$$(1/r) < b - c - (v * s * t)$$

According to mathematics, if any of these values would be 0, g become 0:

v=0 : The employee feels not responsible for the deviation, it was an accident.

s=0 : The employee does not perceive a negative impact for the company

t=0 : The employee is still in the process of decision making.

If 1/"anticipated compliance risk" is lower than the benefit of possible compliance involvement, minus the costs of information and the gap, the employee most-likely will continue on the wrong path without making the situation transparent, as it is easier to give in the temptation to follow the wrong path than to resist it and return to right one.

Also with these factors Compliance can work:

- Responsibility: Workshops can discuss the responsibility of employees, especially regarding approvals and signatures.
- Severity: A good Compliance training is not limited on laws and regulations, but explains also what is behind, like cost of corruption. Further Compliance can be presented as part of the company's sustainability strategy. It is not just important to sell today, but also to sell in the future.

As the flow of time is still no value, which we can influence, the race is on; and Compliance should make it the employee as easy as possible to get reached and support them.

This formula is not meant to be a mathematical equation, but should explain the relation, which have the single factors on each other.

2 THE FRAUD TRIANGLE

Opportunity

Motivation

Rationalization

Can a geometric figure, used already in a 70's theory, still be relevant for us today? As you will see here, especially because of its simplicity Donald Cressey's Fraud Triangle[10] is still is usable for a simple or even more detailed risk assessment.

If you are looking for weak points in your corporate anti-corruption program; motivation, opportunity and rationalization bring it on the point.

---

[10] Crassey, Donald (1973): "Other People's Money: A Study in the Social Psychology of Embezzlement"

2.1 Motivation

What are the drivers behind our actions or why we are working in the company where we are working in? We are living in complicated times and cases like the NSA specialist Edward Snowden show us that the motivation for a fraud (to have no political discussion what is a fraud, we just take the point of view of employer) is not always the money. To understand this better we have to go even more back in time; until the 40s of the last century, but again it is the geometric figure of a triangle: "The Hierarchy of Needs" by the Abraham Maslow. In this original model, also known as his pyramid, he is defining 5 different levels of needs. First the physiological, safety, social and ego needs; then the wish for self-actualization. Hereby we have the general idea that an individual first have to satisfy the needs from a lower level, before it feels the needs from the higher ones, for example first you must have something to eat today, before you want to ensure that you have enough to eat for the whole month. But there are exceptions, a racing driver normally is on the third level of the pyramid and is now in the process to satisfy the ego needs of the fourth level, but this means given up the primary needs for security.[11]

- Self actualization
- Ego   n
- Social   e
- Safety   e
- Physiological   d
             s

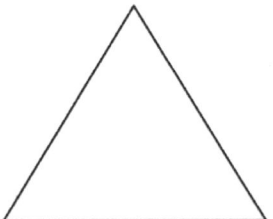

Coming back to our company, we can have a theft out of the pure need for money, based on the basic needs of the first or second level, but it can be based also on the third following level and beyond. Maslow introduced in a later model of his pyramid an even higher level, which he just describes as "transcendence". An incompatibility between the personal values of an employee and the perceived values of the

---

[11] Maslow, Abraham (1943): "A Theory of Human Motivation"

company is leading to an inner dissonance. As the individual feels the need for a positive self-perception on the higher levels, it tries to get its life back into harmony; it can be with a simple leaving of the company or the leaving with a "big bang", like a fraud.

The motivation risk is known, but what can a company do to reduce it? The first step is not the task for a Compliance, legal or internal audit department. Human resources together with the management must understand which the different needs of the employees are, and what would make them happier. As we have learnt this is not automatically a higher loan, but also being part of a community, receiving recognition or living out its personal creativity. Of course each character is different, someone is happy if told what to do, another one wants to have more space to make its own decisions. One employee, might like an office with a window, another one prefers a smaller laptop. Important is that HR and management know and understand their people. Only if we know what our employees need and drive, we can really integrate them into our company.

2.1.1 A sustainability lesson by the Godfather himself

The compliance strategy an important part of sustainability, what is also easy to be explained. If you leave any ethical thoughts aside for a moment, the task of a Compliance department is simple to avoid that the company is engaged in any un-lawful business, which can have a million dollar fine or a black-listing as result; and with this risking the company's prosper future. For this compliance and sustainability are part of the company's middle and long range strategy. The problem hereby, a human being and a company think in another time dimensions. 5 years for a 100 years old company is nothing, but for the employee in 5 years you can be in a complete new situation of life; marriage, new-born baby, house sale, child in high-school or university, etc.

Clean business is important for the company, to be still successful in the market in 10 years, but a lot of employees are not planning that far on the long run. For them the question how to pay the summer holidays can be already on the long run. That is why we have to be aware that a (very) small part of our employees might be motivated to take an ethical short-cut.

Needs are nothing fixed and nothing objective. For example the marketing business spends lots of money not just inform us which new products are out there, but also on the emotional level, make us wanting them, making us aware of needs we maybe not felt before. Emotions and the creation of needs are both, an opportunity and also risk for the corporate compliance.

An employee may not always be fully aware of what is motivating her or him. Group pressure, for example can be a motivational factor. First you may see this as a risk, but you can

The Godfather's advice *"A man who is not a father to his children can never be a real man."*[12] supports us in two ways:

1) Being a father or mother enlarges the employee's scope for the private planning, as now it is not enough to plan for the own life, but also the possibilities for the next generation, at least until end of school and /or university. As more than just one life depends on you, your involvement in the decision makings goes up and the individual in average takes more time to process additional information, before a decision gets made. This reduces the risk that the employees gets rushed into a bad decision.

---

[12] Puzo, Mario (1969): The Godfather

2) Family and children is a center point for the employee. Without this private construction, employees feel less need for private life and in average spend more time in office and business. Such high concentration on your tasks may provoke a "tunnel vision". For this it is imperative that employees take their breaks and have sufficient leisure-time, to relax, get other ideas and, if possible, process experiences and talk with trusted third parties, as a family member.

A company which works with such a philosophy is the Atlanta based fast-food chain "Chick-fil-A". Company founder S. Truett Cathy built up the restaurant chain, which differs from its competitors: All franchisees have to accept that the restaurants stay closed on Sundays. With that the employees and potential clients have the possibility to visit mess and spend quality time with the family. Franchise costs are relative low in relation to other fast food restaurants, but therefor Chick-fil-A expect their franchisees to be active in the local Christian communities and even include their restaurant here, for example offering free breakfasts for the poor or space for learning groups. With this the company not only supports Christian believes, but also get emotional settled employees. Due to Cathy, married workers are more industrious and productive. "If a man can't manage his own life, he can't manage a business." With this philosophy Chick-fil-A not only interviews the potential restaurant operators, but also their spouses and children. Of course with this politics, the company faces also criticism and charges of employment discrimination, but so far, state and federal laws not forbid their company philosophy.[13]

If you enter in one of their restaurants in the US or Brazil, you get the impression that quality, service and cleanness have a higher standard than at the competition. So the decision where to eat and where not, is with the customer. At the end, beside philosophy and values, it reduces the employee risk factor. But if we go back to the beginning it makes clear that such a strategy also not automatically leads to positive

---

[13] Small, Emily (2007): "The Cult of Chick-fil-A"

effects, as Mario Puzo's Mafia had no problems to combine their business with integrity and faith.

2.1.2 Procurement

The procurement department is in all companies one of the risk groups for compliance. But risk should not be seen as something negative. It just means this is a key group, involved in important decisions of the company. For this these people, are not the enemy, quite the opposite, they can be an allied, as later explained.

Procurement employees are not just in Christmas time a preferred target for receiving gifts and presents. Such packages can arrive at the office address, but of course also at their homes. Why this is a problem, why we cannot just be happy for them having a new TV flat screen in their living room?

The answer is that receiving gifts works on two levels. On the conscious one, we see the objective or personal value the gift has for us. This makes the sender looking more sympatric, seem he or she really cares about me and the good business relation we have, with this we assume that we are a strategic client for him and this sustainable idea should be included in his offers. Maybe they are not the cheapest, but having solutions with and good and satisfying quality.

Further, gifts are working on the sub-conscious level; we have received something from another person and so feel that our relation is not anymore in balance. On the third level, the social one, we got a problem. We are feeling being part of a group, but the relation is in risk, if others always giving more than they are receiving, some day they will exclude this individual from the group. As procurement employees in general do not have budget to send gifts to their providers, they are temptation, conscious or sub-conscious, give a preference to the offers from these companies, which gave them a gift before.

Procurement is a key-partner for Compliance, as they are not only a risk group, but on the other hand have to control the other risk groups like Sales or Project Management. In the heat of the moment these two groups are doing the best they can to win the important projects; an enormous pressure, which can lead to ethical blindness. Here enters Procurement and their policies. In general, there is a process in place that a Project Manager cannot take the decision, with which suppliers to work with, but Procurement has to investigate and create several offers from different suppliers; where they together with project management are deciding, which offer will be taken. With this they are not only an independent group, which is involved in procurement process, but they also support with creating a short break and decisions are not being taken in the "heat of the moment".

2.1.3 Compliance Trainings and Communication

The creation of new needs is not always a treat for the Compliance program, quite the opposite; this can be used also for the good. Compliance communication and trainings should not limit their selves to inform about implemented processes and policies, including the consequences the ignoring of them, but going further, motivate the employees and so open the need to work in a transparent and ethical environment. This is, of course, in the more risky regions easier to reach than in transparent ones. If the negative results of corruption are part of your daily life, for example through a bad infrastructure, high prices or bad public school system; it makes the life easier for the Compliance Officer to explain the advantages of a transparent market and region.

To motivate employees, it is imperative that the Compliance training not just answers the question "what" is forbidden, but also explains the "why". This was always relevant, but now even more than ever, as the "Millennials" or "Generation Y" (spoken "why") get a relevant part of today's work-force, as they are born from 1977 to '98. The "Y" has a double-meaning, first as they are following the "Generation X" and second as they want to understand their surroundings. They are in a comfortable situation, as big parts of them have a higher education level and enough financial protection to stay for a limited time without regular income. As consequence they require more personal independence in their work, so that they can create their area of responsibility based on their personal values. With this they confirm Maslow's pyramid. In opposite to earlier generations, thanks to their family background and / or social security, they do not start on the first level of Maslow's Pyramid and require to "earn their living", but have already the third level as their starting point.

This makes it clear that these typical characteristics are based on three factors: 1) financial situation, 2) socialization and 3) technological development.

Similar to known marketing campaigns, Compliance communication and trainings can create or at least foster the employees' needs, attitudes and values. Especially in countries with a higher corruption level this is a big opportunity, as corruption and its costs for society is not just an abstract topic, but experienced by all employees in their daily life, independent from their level inside the company. Further, even if you live in such country, you know from TV / internet / travel other regions with lower corruption levels and these benefits. The Compliance Officer can use this and explain:

Complying with internal guidelines and external laws — lead to → benefits of living in a country with lower corruption level

Of course you have to be honest that his is now easy process, but if you start today, it can be reached in maybe two generations. But smaller results could be reached earlier:

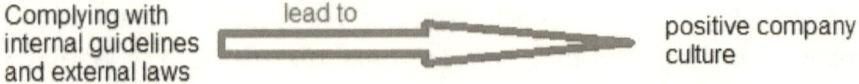

Complying with internal guidelines and external laws — lead to → positive company culture

It is much more motivating to work for a clean company, not only as you support with this the general transparency of the market and society, but also it has direct personal benefits, as you can advance with your career thanks to your results and not to your friendships.

Taking individuals out of their known surrounding and put them into a new, unknown and as hostile perceived surrounding leads to a "loss of control"-effect, where humans tend to not act anymore or their personal values, but try all kind of behavior to get out of this uncomfortable situation, it is important to explain inside the Compliance trainings and workshops that everybody is important and every single person is responsible and has to support Compliance, if necessary also with the usage of the whistleblower hotline. Such hotlines should be presented not as a medium to report suspicious cases, but furthermore a tool to protect the company and surely more than 99% of the honest and hardworking employees; then one thing is for sure, 1 bad employee alone can destroy the work of thousand good ones. So what has to be avoided is the by-stander effect as often seen in the traffic, but to have employees, who really would start acting, if needed. Yes you can!

An effective Compliance program is founded on the core values of the company and not just has an external effect, but also internally has to ensure the right culture and tone from the top. One of its basic messages must be that everybody is responsible for its own actions; there can be no more excuses that my manager told me to do this or that. Everybody is a part of compliance and he or she gets the advice to do something, what is against the company's values and policies, or even the law. There must be an open atmosphere to discuss this between employee and manager. If the your manager insists to execute this order, you not just have the possibility to use a whistleblower hotline, but it is also your responsibility to do so! This philosophy should ensure that there is a positive and democratic work atmosphere, where everybody has the same chances to grow and develop him or herself. That this is working, compliance already starts in the recruiting process.

Not just that human resources must ensure to hire an ethical person, but also an active "success-seeker" instead of the more passive "avoider of failures".

Be aware that as Compliance Officer you are also a sales-person. It is impossible to control the total of the employees all the time. So you depend on that the people are "buying" from you the idea that integrity and ethics is important and that we all should act on the relevant business conduct guidelines. Based on this philosophy, all employees of the company are your internal clients, and you are offering a service for them. For your trainings you might like to use also some of the classical sales tactics, like "foot in the door" or "door in the face".

- "Foot in the door": This sales technique is based on an a classic experiment by Freedman and Fraser.[14] The idea is to start with a small request, where the requester is relatively sure that the individual will agree to. For example, if he or she can have a glass of water. After this you continue with a bigger question and continue until you reached the question, what you really want to ask, as if the potential client want to buy the product.

- "door in the face": Practically the opposite of the earlier technique. Here you start with a big request, where you must assume that the other person cannot agree to. Then you change strategy and continue with a small request until you have a question, where the other person finally will agree to. This is the request where you originally wanted to have the agreement to.[15]

Due to statistics, both strategies have higher success rate, as if the requester directly would have asked the original question to the individual.

---

[14] Freedman, J.L. / Fraser, S.C. (1966): "Compliance without pressure: The foot-in-the-door technique."
[15] Cialdini, R.B. / Vincent, J.E. / Lewis, S.K. / Catalan, J. / Wheeler, D. / Darby, B.L. (1975): "Reciprocal concessions procedure for inducing compliance: the door-in-the-face technique."

2.1.4 The Risk of the Small Temptation

Joseph Fouché (1759 – 1820) was Minister of Police under Napoleon Bonaparte and based on his experience he told once: *"If it is said that a person in incorruptible, I ask myself involuntarily whether one has offered him enough."*

But it is really so easy? Could it be just the other way around?

In most of cases temptation does not come directly with the suitcase full of money, but a rather small piece. This is similar the "foot-in-the-door technique."[16] Its key-message, people are most likely to agree to a big request, if they get first asked for a small one.

A small request has in general an insignificant meaning for the individual, so that no detailed inner-personal decision making process gets started and a regarding action executed. For corruption this small request can be a facilitation payment or another low illegal payment. The problem can be solved with the help of some few Dollars. As the

---

[16] Freedman, J.L. / Fraser, S.C. (1966): "Compliance without pressure: The foot-in-the-door technique"

sum is insignificant for the potential payer, there starts no thinking about the side effects, as supporting corrupt infrastructure or committing a legal crime (as facilitation payments are illegal due to most local laws). The payer does not create a sense of guilt, as a simple "everybody does it" calms the individual.

Later on the way the employee can face a bigger request, as for example, a kick-back payment. Now the inner-personal decision making process gets activated and the individual collects all reasons for and against paying the bribe. One argument which comes up now is the memory that an illegal payment had been made before. Nothing happened, no legal consequence, nor did it seem that is has hurt someone. Due to the memory, the individual assumes that he or she has in general a positive attitude to bribe someone. This does not automatically lead to the decision to pay the higher bribe, but could be an important step to it.

As the risk is known, it is up to the company to implement counter measures. It must be clear to all employees, not only the typical Compliance risk groups, that there is zero tolerance for facilitation payments. Further, employees must understand which costs of corruption are behind even small bribes. With this knowledge the individual presents a higher involvement into the topic and even a request for a small illegal payment will trigger a detailed inner-personal decision making process.

2.1.5 Focus on the Vision

Another possibility to ensure clean business and sustainability is to go back to the founding hours of the company and to the original visions and ideas, as it was not all about the money, but to make the founder's dream come alive, as Enzo Ferrari said: *"What we do here is elite work."*

The mentioned "elite work" is not just a sign of respect from the employees to the employer. Furthermore it is a sign of respect of the whole company towards its clients. By these means are the same trust concepts valid as between two persons. If the client does not understand the offered product, not esteems it or, even worse in the business-to-business-relation, asks for improper discounts, the supplier loses the respect for the potential client. When negotiations are only about the money, elite work cannot get maintained. Not only because the invested time does not pay, but because dedication does not get appreciated. Positive recognition is an important motivational factor. Employees need it from the management, but also to receive it from the customer. This is another reason why it is imperative to have an internal control and compliance system, because if parts of the company, as sales or procurement would start doing business in a improper matter, for example with giving or receiving bribes, on the long run this behavior would spread out in the whole company and even affect the production unit. As they would see that their products do no not receive any more the wanted appreciation, as the client's procurement department chooses them based on personal benefits (bribe), it is impossible for these engineers and factory workers to motivate themselves and produce elite work.

Further if we understand his philosophy and actions, we can see that most of this did not lost any meaning and Enzo is still an inspiration for today's managers and leaders; for the sustainability of the company and the benefit of most employees. For all employees? Definitely not, as history showed that he was indeed a leader with edges. But this is not different from two other celebrated leaders as Steve Jobs or Richard Branson. Enzo was aware of his weaknesses, but could say that he always stayed faithful to his own philosophy.

2.2 Opportunity

2.2.1 Temptations

As the famous Irish poet and writer Oscar Wilde once said, *"I can resist everything except temptation"*. If we take his picture of the human being and we are for real with our integrity and ethics approach, we cannot limit our self to the prevention approach, but we have to have an efficient detection system. This means not that we just want to control our people in the risky areas, but also that we taking away temptation from them. "Everybody hast his prices", another philosophy, which is not that new, as we now it already from ... and ... Hereby giving in to a temptation does not automatically mean that the employee is selfish; this can happen also based on an altruistic motive. For example a brutal decision: " Your wife needs and urgent surgery, but you are at the bottom of the waiting list. But with the help of a 1.000 USD bribe, she can move up the list and gets this life-saving treatment." An ethics dilemma.

But we do not even have to go to such extremes. In the several cases of "good people doing bad things", employees have been actively involved into corruption not for a direct or non-direct benefit, but because they have thought, it was in the best interest of the company. Even if such cases would be detected early and it will not lead to an external case, quite probable the employee would be separated from the company. A not non-important cost factor, because the company loses experience (which maybe will go with the ex-employee to the direct competency) and have to build up a new employee. For this important not just to have regarding policies in place, but also communicate in a clear and direct way that bribes have no place in the company. This should avoid that employees identify an opportunity, where in reality is none.

Also normally there are more than 99% of honest and employees working for the company. But less than 1% of people can destroy the work of them all. Depending investigated cases, the corruption was sometimes more and sometimes less systematic in a company; but nevertheless we are still speaking about small groups and in most cases not of the majority of the employees. But that was the result? Fines and additional costs of several million US-Dollar per company. As fines should be higher than the former improper gained advantages, this is money, which is now missing the company. Missing for research and development, marketing strategies, etc. until salaries. Also in the time after the knowledge of potential case, it is an image problem for the company, which makes it more difficult to see its projects and products. But furthermore, if there are investigations, employees are unsure what to do and what responsibilities to take, this affects the decision making process and the company became less efficient for a period. As seen in the motivation chapter, employees gets demotivated, because they are not proud anymore to tell their friends and family, where they are working at. They not like anymore the group they are in and may like to change this, with taking other job opportunities.

So controls are taking away the burden of temptation from the employee, which means Compliance controls are not only a necessary part of an integrity culture, they are also ethical. For this controls are something positive and should be communicated like this in the company's Compliance trainings.

One of highest temptations in business live can be facilitation payments. First of all, because employees not face them in their normal office surrounding, but mostly on travels and in public offices. So the situation is assumed as a "away match" and the rules here are made by the home team. Due to Julian B. Rotter's "locus of control"-theory from 1954, individuals perceive situations, where they are get asked for a bribe or facilitation payment as a situation, where not themselves have the control, but the public official. It is an unknown state, where learned behaviors (for example if an employee from a low risk country is facing this situation in an high risk one) are not getting any desired results. Then the individual tries nearly randomly other behaviors, which might or might not be based on its personal values. As the person wants to get out this unpleasant situation as fast as possible, a relative low payment is a welcome solution.

As we speak he normally about values, for which the employee normally not asks the company for reimbursement, classic compliance controls are not working here.

The best what a company can do here is to work on the values and so create a kind of ethical vaccination. This important, because in most of the countries a facilitation payment is legally defined as a bribe, so can bring the company into trouble.

Another reason why a control system is ethically is, it takes away the objective and / or subjective "pressure to be corrupt". In our business life we are always in competency, this can be with our colleagues and, of course, also with other companies. What is expected from us is winning. If there are no clear rules in the game, you cannot be sure what your management is expecting from you, stay by the legal rules or maybe also to include some smaller or bigger "strategic foul", if needed? With the implementation of a value- and control-based compliance system, it is clear to all employees, what is expected from you and what not. As shown before, the individual acts now in a known surrounding, what is more pleasant and for the whole company should lead to a better working atmosphere.

Also the opportunity as part of the fraud triangle should not always be seen as a risk factor, it can be also quite the opposite; there can be opportunities to do wrong, but there can be also opportunities to speak up and do the right thing. This should be fostered while making it as easy and secure as possible to speak up. One example here is the whistleblower hotline. On the hand it brings an unpredictable element to the control system, because even with the best knowledge of the internal control system and how to bypass it, you can never be sure, if maybe some colleague has seen you or even a "partner in crime" wants to step out and so informs the management. On the other hand, the anonymity of a well-known telephone-number or email-address makes it easy for an employee to stand up, because there not have to be invested much time in report and the anonymity guarantees that there are later no sanctions against the reporter.

Employees learn the Compliance culture via different learning methods. The classical "instructionalism", the "cognitivism" and the "conditioning".

- The best example for instrucionalism is a Compliance training, could be online or also in person. In a quite one-way communication the Compliance Officer tells the group, what is allowed and what is forbidden, incl. all the necessary processes and policies.
- An interactive workshop is an example for cognitism. The Compliance Officer discusses topics and cases with the group. For this the employees not just receive the pre-made opinion from the instructor, but their selves are analyzing the problem and with group discussion coming theirselves to the wanted result. Employees are much more involved in the topic in comparison to the simple instructional training, so that the topics and results are also much better memorized.
- Conditioning can be also seen as learning by doing, could be your own doing, or observed one. Quite similar to Pavlo's dog, people learn with action and re-action. Simply said, an employee steals 100 USD from the company; the control system is working and he gets caught and separated. For this individual the control was behind the action, but his colleagues see this case and learn that steeling means automatic separation. The control is working preventive. On the other the company has to work sensibly with its whistleblower hotline. In a lot of cultures people are sceptic against these kind of hotlines, so the slightest rumor that a whistleblower got sanctions against a potential

Compliance case, potential future whistleblowers will think two, three or even more times, if they really want to use this tool.

As the whistleblower hotline is one of the most important tools of each Compliance system; number, functions and anonymity must be mentioned in all Compliance trainings with additional use of other communication channels (for example posters). As people may feel skeptical against this tool, the more often they hear that it is safe to use and important for all, the more they will believe in this. This might be a more boring part in the training or workshop, but as no compliance system can and want guarantee a 100% control, it is necessary.[17]

To avoid a bystander effect, trainings should point out that ethics and compliance are everybody's responsibility. The employees are not a grey and aninoums group of people, but each person has its own personality and importance for the company. So everybody is not just part of the group, but individually important. For this everybody can make a change, with using the anonymous whistleblower hotline, you not even have to take a risk for this.

2.2.2 Illusion of Control: From Van Gogh to Atari

Dutch post-impressionist painter Vincent van Gogh (1873-1890) said once: *"I put my heart and my soul into my work, and have lost my mind in the process."* More than hundred years later, this sounds like the perfect description for a phenomenon, what we call "ethical blindness".

"Formally, ethical blindness can be defined as the temporary inability of a decision maker to see the ethical dimension of a decision at stake."[1]

---

[17] Illusion-of-truth effect

Due to the combination of different psychological pressures, the employee develops a tunnel vision, or as a German proverb says, because of all the trees it is impossible to see the forest. Some of the pressures include, but are not limited to, peer pressure, role behavior or time pressure.

Another risk factor, which can lead to Ethical Blindness, is the "illusion of control"-effect. Depending on a person's character, employees overestimate their possibility to control a situation. This is especially true for "success seekers", they tend to overestimate their own abilities and underestimate the risks of the situation. For the "failure avoiders" it is the other way around. Thanks to self-selection the first group of people will try to get more risky tasks with the goal that they can prove their selves and advance faster in their career.[2]

In the early 1980's the hard-and-software company Atari was the favorite of the US stock market and the Silicone Valley. It was the first company who presented their programmers as games designers and celebrated them similar to rock stars. A concept what got copied by other competitors like Activision, who printed the name of their programmers directly under the game title, similar to movie posters. Howard Scott Warshaw was one of Atari's most talented game designers. He created the Indiana Jones game "Raiders of the Lost Ark" and "Yars' Revenge". Both had been very successful products, especially the second, as it became Atari's best-selling game, which not had been based on a license (as Pac Man).

"E.T. – the Extra Terrestrial" became a movie sensation in '82 and Atari's mother concern Warner Brothers had been keen to participate in the global merchandising. Finally director Steven Spielberg agreed on the license for a video-game. The problem: It was already summer and it was necessary to develop a game in just 5 weeks, if the company wanted to aim for the attractive Christmas business. Thanks to his successful earlier games, Warshaw had enough self-affirmation to take on this task. Never before a game was finished in such a short time and he did the impossible with delivering on time. Unfortunately the quality of the game-play was not as expected and the game became known in history as the "worst game of all times".[3]

To be honest, it was a disappointing game, but definitively not the worst of all time, not even Atari's. (*I remember that I received the game for Christmas and liked it at that time. Even if it was difficult, it was not impossible, as I completed once to build the telephone, so that the big space ship came to pick up E.T.*) Nevertheless it was perceived as this, also as there was such a huge gap between the quality of the movie and the relating game. The end of '82 became a turning point for Atari and the whole videogame industry. Finally in '84 Warner sold Atari to Jack Tramel, who restructured the company to develop "the next big thing", the home computer.

Warshaw took on an impossible task to create a high quality game in such a short period and with this destroyed a must-win project. This was not the only factor for the company's downfall, but nevertheless an important one, as it seriously damaged the Atari image and reputation. Another important factor for this was the underestimated success of the home computer, and here first of all, the C64.

As a lesson learnt, it is mandatory to have an efficient risk control process implemented in the company. A project is always an opportunity, but if the adequate execution is not ensured; integrity should tell the company not to participate. Consequences can be a negative impact on the company, including fines and loss of reputation. Honesty is a sign of respect, not just between individuals, but also companies.

A positive corporate culture presumed, "success seekers" must be included into an internal group. With this, decisions are not taken alone, but jointly, "failure avoiders" included. Smartphones, tools and apps can reduce the "perceived isolation" of sales employees and project managers. Even if not office, you are always connect with your decision group. Compliance workshops can work as an "ethical vaccination", as the fostering of knowledge, values and attitudes can lower the risk of Ethical Blindness.

2.3 Rationalization

2.3.1 Corruption & Behavior

The complete group of employees is impossible to be controlled by 100%. Also it should be avoided to even make the effort to do so, because the only perfectly controlled company is the closed company. It has to found a natural balance between values and controls. In the ideal work employees are doing the right thing, because they believe in it; and not because the company has a control system in place. This sounds simple, but in most of world's countries corruption is learnt directly through the parents, as bribery, corruption, usage of piracy and relations is a common way to act in given situations; what could be interpreted as part of a local culture. If you have learnt that bribery is a successful, companies have a risk that these employees may use this learnt behavior also to carry on in the business life. For this a good training cannot limit itself just talking about laws and policies, but has to foster or even change the ethical values. This is not just important for the offices in "high risk countries", but also for trainings in countries, with a low corruption level. This for two reasons:

- Low corruption risk still means there is a corruption risk! For employees, which are not grown up a corrupt ambient, a situation, where they get asked for a bribe is completely new and outside all known scenarios. In this situation of a loss of control, employees are tempted to take the first and easiest exit ("paying the bribe") to get out of this unknown and uncomfortable situation.
- We are living in a globalized world, where it is part of our world, also to travel to other countries, cultures and continents. Here employees are getting faced easily with facilitation payments or even corruption.

For this a good compliance training always has to prepare the people for such situations. Role-plays, guidance and contact information for such unusual situations will make them feel more comfortable and self-confidant. With this the training is working as like an "ethical vaccination".

Corruption is learnt from early age. We sit in the car, while our father or mother got stopped by the police. If we are living in a country with a higher corruption level we may see now our dad or mom taking out some money and the topic got solved. We saw an example of operant conditioning: problem, behavior, reward.

Some years later we got more independent from our parents and are now ourselves in the role of Pavlov's dog. As we had no experience of our own, we copied our parents: problem, behavior, reward. This can get so far that our behavior gets a reflex (classical conditioning), even if there will be no reward anymore. For example, we drove too fast and the police stopped us. We took out some money, but the policeman (or woman) politely refused to take it.

We keep our behavior; it does not lead to desired result, but also has no negative consequence. The only way that we chance our behavior would be the introduction of a punishment. Again we drove too fast and got stopped by the friendly policeman (or woman). We took out our money, but this time no polite refusal, but we had to pay a fine for offering a bribe. At once we learnt from this and would the next time change our behavior. Hopefully now are complying with the speed limits.

Important is the expectation of the outcome, which is determined by two factors the possibility of the outcome and the outcome itself. For example you can have 5 possible business cases.

- Offer (Price + Quality) = 100 USD
- Offer (Price + Quality) = 100 USD
- Offer (Price + Quality) = 100 USD
- Offer (Price + Quality) = 100 USD
- Offer (Price + Quality) = 100 USD
- Total: 500 USD

As alternative you can support your offer with a bribe:

- Offer (Price + Quality + Bribe) = 200 USD
- Offer (Price + Quality + Bribe) = 200 USD
- Offer (Price + Quality + Bribe) = 200 USD
- Offer (Price + Quality + Bribe) = 200 USD
- Offer (Price + Quality + Bribe) = -200 USD (getting caught)
- Total: 600 USD

From a pure economic point of view (and not including the general costs of corruption), the second alternative is more attractive. Paying a bribe or not is no question of culture, but calculation. If want to foster ethical behavior, as clean business or correct payment of taxes, you have two possibilities.

1. Raise the fines: If getting caught means -400 USD instead of -200, the total changes to 400 USD. Inferior to the perceived outcome of clean business. If the fines raise to 800 USD, the total outcome would be 0 and with this a serious threat to the sustainability of the business.
2. Raise the controls: If you are getting caught 3 times, instead of only once, your total would change from 600 USD to -200 USD. Again a serious threat to the future of the company.

Humans do these calculations, but of course do not stay completely to the mathematic rules. If you got caught once, you perceive in many cases the general possibility of getting caught higher than it is. The same is valid for the other way around. If you did not get caught, you are tempt to perceive the risk lower than it is in reality.

That this is not just a nice concept got confirmed by Raymund Fisman and Edward Miguel with their study: "Corruption, Norms, and Legal Enforcement: Evidence from Diplomatic Parking Tickets"

2.3.2 Corruption and Company Behavior

Corruption is a cost factor for the society or as Transparency International chairman Jose Ugaz said: "Corruption is a tax that is paid by the poorest in our countries." But what about the companies? Corruption is also for them an additional tax?

The World Bank Group elaborates an annual index, which ranks 189 countries, based on their ease of doing business in relation to the local regulatory environment. In the 2014 list we find Singapore, New Zealand, Hong Kong, Denmark and South Korea on the first five positions. Two of these countries, Denmark and New Zealand, are also in the Top Five of Transparency International's Corruption Perception Index 2014. If we compare the complete country listings and calculate the correlation coefficient, we get 0.79 as result. As this formula creates a value from 0 to 1, our results presents a strong statistic relation between the two indices.

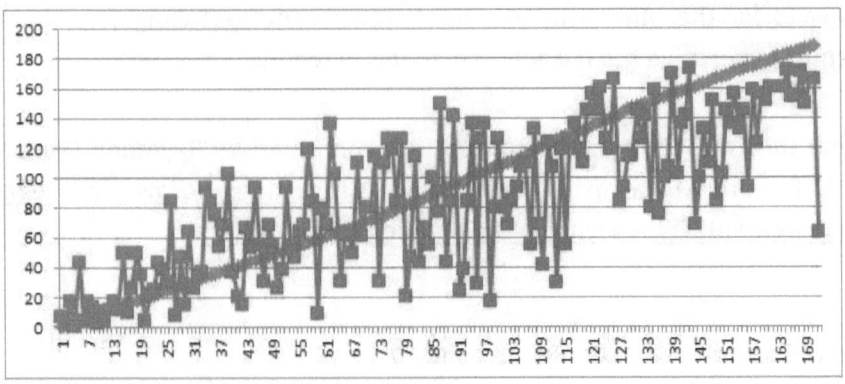

The graphics presents the "ease to do business"-index as linear graph and additionally the TI-CPI, both from 2014.

Such a relation can be explained as in countries with a higher corruption level, an adequate execution of laws is not guaranteed by following the processes. Often governmental officials ask for bribes or at least a facilitation payment (interpreted as bribe according to most local laws).

Further it means that bribing often leads to success on the short run: the wished outcome gets achieved and thanks to general impunity, the chance of getting caught ("casino risk") is relative low.

The "homo economicus" is following the direction, which seems to create the highest profit. This can mean giving in to the temptation to pay a bribe or going the hard way, denying the informal payment, use the legal opportunities and escalate the topic or as worst case, give up this particular business. All possible decisions mean that conducting business is complicated, including legal and financial risks.

The correlation shows a strong relation between the perceived corruption level and the difficulty to conduct business in the country. For the case that both values present a difference, there is the pressure to come together at some point:

- Corruption > Difficulty: As paying bribes does not seem to be necessary to conduct business, the society has the opportunity to use the available transparency to combat the local corruption level. On the other hand, corrupt institutions have an interest to keep the status quo and will try to raise bureaucracy to ensure their illegal position of power.

- Difficulty > Corruption: Bureaucracy can provoke corruption, as employees and companies might start to look for "short-cuts" through the legal jungle. As the corruption level is still relative low, it is mandatory to reduce inefficient regulations to achieve a smooth and legal way to conduct business.

It is not possible to predict which of the two sides will be stronger. To reduce the corruption level, a political consensus is required, beyond the boundaries of political borders. An active society and independent journalism is requirement for this. Against this are efficient informal networks, which try to protect their-selves.

Difficulty = Corruption: A relative equilibrium is reached. As described above, the perceived corruption level is no result of a culture, but learnt. This insight gets fostered by the idea that the country is not a closed group, but includes temporary players; foreigners which do not have a problem to adapt to the relative equilibrium.

As the country is not a closed group, an external factor pressures the local status quo. Laws as the US "Foreign Corrupt Practices Act" or the "United Kingdom Bribery Act" evolve a global responsibility for companies to comply with, independent if they act in- or out-side the US / UK. For this companies not just have to comply with local laws, but with the strict US and UK one, including the risk of their potential fines.

With this the absolute equilibrium lays at perfect ease to conduct business together with zero corruption: low temptation (corruption) with low motivation (bureaucracy). This effect gets fostered as through globalization the group members are in interchange with others. Even if you live most of your time in a country with a higher corruption level, you have the possibility to stay temporally (holidays, work, university, etc.) in a country with a lower one. Here people enjoy the results of transparency and less inefficient bureaucracy. With a changed mindset they come back and demand a similar environment for their own region, groups and companies.

As the ease of doing business depends on the local corruption level, we can say that corruption is not only a tax for citizens, but also for companies. As countries are in a global competition for foreign investments, perceived corruption is a negative factor to attract such investments. At the end the sufferer are again the people, as adequate jobs are missing.

2.3.3 Illusion of Truth

Hasher, Goldstein and Toppino discovered this cognitive bias in 1977. It can be resumed as that people believe that information is correct, if they are exposed repeatedly.[18]

As all psychology, this can be used for the good or the bad. It can be used to repeatedly communicate wrong information with the goal that the receivers start believing in it. But it could be used also to communicate the truth and positive values.

The company's communication department has to find a compromise between repeating relevant messages and avoiding an information overflow. Also has the message be aligned with management behavior. As non-verbal communication beats the verbal one, an adequate tone

---

[18] Hasher, L / Goldstein, D. / Toppino, T. (1977): "Frequency and the conference of referential validity"

from the top and all levels is imperative!

Further communication should be as interactive as possible to involve all employees. This supports to foster the company values. Often an individual is not directly aware of his or her values, for this is dependent to watch him- or her-self. By recognize one's actions and listen to one's words, people assume what drivers, attitudes and values led to the watched behavior. If the company communication can reach to let employee's repeat relevant messages, they will assume from their own watched behavior what they values and attitudes are. In this process, these values will be adapted and in future decisions as decision base taken.

3 EVOLUTION OF THE TRIANGLE

As criminologist he developed the triangle to explain criminal behavior, but as sociologist he did much more, he created a simple model to explain human behavior in groups. Motivation, rationalization and opportunity define which conditions must be given to provoke non-conformal behavior of single participants inside a group. On the other hand the triangle identifies which areas to focus on to prevent possible wrong-doings and implement adequate counter-measures.

In a political context this can become dangerous, as it could be used to manipulate group-members and -dynamics, but, for example, in a company it can and should be used to foster a positive corporate culture, in favor of the company and its employees. In the previous chapter we discussed the specific risks and opportunities. Even without knowing the company's risks in detail, you can "vaccinate" employees against actual and future temptations:

- Motivation: A positive corporate culture fosters the employees' engagement and lowers the risk that someone would jeopardize this.
- Rationalization: If employees understand the relations between business success and sustainability, the consequences of individual behavior and the costs of corruption, they would find less possibilities to argue in favor of a fraud.
- Opportunity: Due to a quote by an anonymous author, every individual fights its own battles. As we know that employees face different pressures, for this the company should keep temptations as low as possible. A robust Compliance system reduces opportunities to a minimum. As the risks are known, it is up to the company to implement and foster an internal system, which works on the prevention to have an open corporate culture to rationalize the right behavior, motivate the employees and closes potential opportunities. This is not a one-

time, but ongoing task, as not only markets and products are changing, but also humans. A regular testing and adaption of the internal Compliance system is imperative.

4 BIBLIOGRAHPY

- Brundtland, H.: " Our common future", 1987, part of the Brundtlandreport
- Cialdini, R.B. / Vincent, J.E. / Lewis, S.K. / Catalan, J. / Wheeler, D. / Darby, B.L. (1975): "Reciprocal concessions procedure for inducing compliance: the door-in-the-face technique."
- Crassey, Donald (1973): "Other People's Money: A Study in the Social Psychology of Embezzlement"
- Dreher, Axel / Herzfeld, Thomas (2005): "The Economic Costs of Corruption: A Survey and New Evidence
- Freedman, J.L. / Fraser, S.C. (1966): "Compliance without pressure: The foot-in-the-door technique"
- Gutenberg, Erich (1979): "Grundlagen der Betriebswirtschaftslehre, Band 1: Die Produktion"
- Hasher, L / Goldstein, D. / Toppino, T. (1977): "Frequency and the conference of referential validity"
- Maslow, Abraham (1943): "A Theory of Human Motivation"
- Mauro, Paulo (1997): „Why worry about Corruption?"
- Murray, Matthew / Spalding (2015): "Freedom from Official Corruption as a Human Right": http://www.brookings.edu/~/media/research/files/papers/2015/01/27-freedom-corruption-human-right-murray-spalding/murray-and-spalding_v06.pdf
- Puzo, Mario (1969": "The Godfather"
- Rand, Ayn (1957): "Atlas Shrugged"
- Small, Emily (2007): "The Cult of Chick-fil-A": http://www.forbes.com/forbes/2007/0723/080.html
- Sustainable Governance Indicators (2014): "Quality of Democracy": http://www.sgi-

network.org/2014/Democracy/Quality_of_Democracy
- Transparency International (2014): "Corruption Perception Index": http://www.transparency.org/cpi2014/results

5 ABOUT THE AUTHOR

Patrick Henz started his career in the Corporate Information Office and Compliance at the end of 2007, when he was responsible for the implementation of the Siemens Anti-Corruption program in Mexico and several Central American and Caribbean countries. Together with these tasks, he gained valuable insights into global Compliance programs, with a focus on Latin America. Since 2009 in his role as Compliance Officer he is responsible for an effective Compliance program; based on identification, protection, detection, response & recovery and combined with integrity, respect, passion & sustainability . With these means, he defines Compliance as pro-active function, being perceived as guardian, expert and facilitator. The focus is on information to ensure adequate behavior, not only of the human employee, but Artificial Intelligence included.

This means the regular planning and execution of Compliance Risk Assessments and further global reviews. According an effective sustainability strategy, where Compliance plays a key role, he actively promotes the idea at university workshops and conferences (including the ACI Compliance Boot-Camp 2013, '16 and '17 in Houston). Doing so, he became two times President of Honor of Marcus Evans' Latin-American Corporate Compliance Conference 2011 and 2012 in Mexico City, panelist at The Economist Mexico Summit 2015, the 3rd Annual Third Party Risk Management & Oversight Summit 2018 and co-founder of the Ethics & Compliance Forum Mexico, including editor and co-author of the Ethics & Compliance Manual, published in April 2014.

Since 2013 he lives and works in Atlanta, USA.

"An inspiration for managers, leaders and everybody who is interested in Enzo Ferrari's life."

Born 1898 in the Northern-Italian city of Modena, Enzo Ferrari lived his dream and founded the world's most famous sports car manufacturer. This book analyzes how he achieved his goals by what are considered to be modern concepts. Or were leadership theories, emotional intelligence, business ethics, client orientation and sustainability already guiding principles of business in the beginning of the last century.

In his own words, and drawing several parallels to Italian history, he thought he was living in the wrong time. But taking off Il Commendatore's sunglasses, this book presents him as a surprisingly modern leader, who, conscious or not, acted conform the latest business and leadership models, confirmed by key decisions of his company, including the racing-team.

The book not only uses racing decisions and car development as examples, including many photos, but sets them in relation to Enzo's personal business philosophy.

www.ingramcontent.com/pod-product-compliance
Lightning Source LLC
Chambersburg PA
CBHW021415170526
45164CB00002B/659